BALLADS AND POEMS

1915-1930

WORKS OF

STEPHEN VINCENT BENÉT

❧

THE BEGINNING OF WISDOM

FIVE MEN AND POMPEY

JOHN BROWN'S BODY

YOUNG PEOPLE'S PRIDE

HEAVENS AND EARTH

SPANISH BAYONET

YOUNG ADVENTURE

JEAN HUGUENOT

TIGER JOY

BALLADS AND POEMS
1915-1930

BALLADS

and POEMS

1915·1930

STEPHEN VINCENT
⌊BENÉT

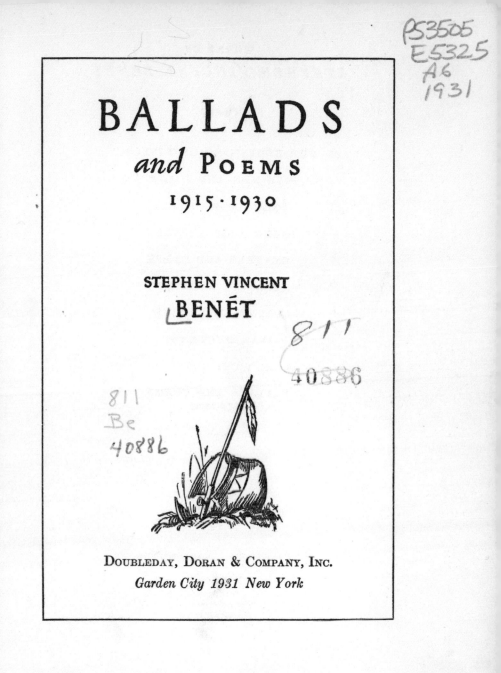

DOUBLEDAY, DORAN & COMPANY, INC.

Garden City 1931 New York

PRINTED AT THE *Country Life Press*, GARDEN CITY, N. Y., U. S. A.

TO ROSEMARY

If you were gone afar,
And lost the pattern
Of all your delightful ways,
And the web undone,
How would one make you anew,
From what dew and flowers,
What burning and mingled atoms,
Under the sun?

Not from too-satin roses,
Or those rare blossoms,
Orchids, scentless and precious
As precious stone.
But out of lemon-verbena,
Rose-geranium,
These alone.

Not with running horses,
Or Spanish cannon,
Organs, voiced like a lion,
Clamor and speed.
But perhaps with old music-boxes,

Young, tawny kittens,
Wild-strawberry-seed.

Even so, it were more
Than a god could compass
To fashion the body merely,
The lovely shroud.
But then—ah, how to recapture
That evanescence,
The fire that cried in pure crystal
Out of its cloud!

NOTE

This book is, in the main, a selection from three earlier books of verse, all now out of print. Some new poems have been added and certain old ones altered, though not materially—one cannot rewrite, after fifteen years, without changing the work completely. The earliest poems in this book were written in 1915, the latest in 1930.

"The Island and the Fire" was read, as the Phi Beta Kappa poem, before the Harvard chapter, June, 1930.

S. V. B.

New York City, 1930

CONTENTS

ix

x

xi

I AMERICAN NAMES

AMERICAN NAMES

I HAVE fallen in love with American names,
The sharp names that never get fat,
The snakeskin-titles of mining-claims,
The plumed war-bonnet of Medicine Hat,
Tucson and Deadwood and Lost Mule Flat.

Seine and Piave are silver spoons,
But the spoonbowl-metal is thin and worn,
There are English counties like hunting-tunes
Played on the keys of a postboy's horn,
But I will remember where I was born.

I will remember Carquinez Straits,
Little French Lick and Lundy's Lane,
The Yankee ships and the Yankee dates
And the bullet-towns of Calamity Jane.
I will remember Skunktown Plain.

[3]

I will fall in love with a Salem tree
And a rawhide quirt from Santa Cruz,
I will get me a bottle of Boston sea
And a blue-gum nigger to sing me blues.
I am tired of loving a foreign muse.

Rue des Martyrs and Bleeding-Heart-Yard,
Senlis, Pisa, and Blindman's Oast,
It is a magic ghost you guard
But I am sick for a newer ghost,
Harrisburg, Spartanburg, Painted Post.

Henry and John were never so
And Henry and John were always right?
Granted, but when it was time to go
And the tea and the laurels had stood all night,
Did they never watch for Nantucket Light?

I shall not rest quiet in Montparnasse.
I shall not lie easy at Winchelsea.
You may bury my body in Sussex grass,
You may bury my tongue at Champmédy.
I shall not be there. I shall rise and pass.
Bury my heart at Wounded Knee.

THE BALLAD
OF WILLIAM SYCAMORE

(1790–1871)

My father, he was a mountaineer,
His fist was a knotty hammer;
He was quick on his feet as a running deer,
And he spoke with a Yankee stammer.

My mother, she was merry and brave,
And so she came to her labor,
With a tall green fir for her doctor grave
And a stream for her comforting neighbor.

And some are wrapped in the linen fine,
And some like a godling's scion;
But I was cradled on twigs of pine
In the skin of a mountain lion.

And some remember a white, starched lap
And a ewer with silver handles;
But I remember a coonskin cap
And the smell of bayberry candles.

[5]

The cabin logs, with the bark still rough,
And my mother who laughed at trifles,
And the tall, lank visitors, brown as snuff,
With their long, straight squirrel-rifles.

I can hear them dance, like a foggy song,
Through the deepest one of my slumbers,
The fiddle squeaking the boots along
And my father calling the numbers.

The quick feet shaking the puncheon-floor,
And the fiddle squealing and squealing,
Till the dried herbs rattled above the door
And the dust went up to the ceiling.

There are children lucky from dawn till dusk,
But never a child so lucky!
For I cut my teeth on "Money Musk"
In the Bloody Ground of Kentucky!

When I grew tall as the Indian corn,
My father had little to lend me,
But he gave me his great, old powder-horn
And his woodsman's skill to befriend me.

With a leather shirt to cover my back,
And a redskin nose to unravel
Each forest sign, I carried my pack
As far as a scout could travel.

Till I lost my boyhood and found my wife,
A girl like a Salem clipper!
A woman straight as a hunting-knife
With eyes as bright as the Dipper!

We cleared our camp where the buffalo feed,
Unheard-of streams were our flagons;
And I sowed my sons like the apple-seed
On the trail of the Western wagons.

They were right, tight boys, never sulky or slow,
A fruitful, a goodly muster.
The eldest died at the Alamo.
The youngest fell with Custer.

The letter that told it burned my hand.
Yet we smiled and said, "So be it!"
But I could not live when they fenced the land,
For it broke my heart to see it.

I saddled a red, unbroken colt
And rode him into the day there;
And he threw me down like a thunderbolt
And rolled on me as I lay there.

The hunter's whistle hummed in my ear
As the city-men tried to move me,
And I died in my boots like a pioneer
With the whole wide sky above me.

[7]

Now I lie in the heart of the fat, black soil,
Like the seed of a prairie-thistle;
It has washed my bones with honey and oil
And picked them clean as a whistle.

And my youth returns, like the rains of Spring,
And my sons, like the wild-geese flying;
And I lie and hear the meadow-lark sing
And have much content in my dying.

Go play with the towns you have built of blocks,
The towns where you would have bound me!
I sleep in my earth like a tired fox,
And my buffalo have found me.

THE HEMP

I. The Planting of the Hemp

CAPTAIN HAWK *scourged ciean the seas*
(Black is the gap below the plank)
From the Great North Bank to the Caribbees.
(Down by the marsh the hemp grows rank).

His fear was on the seaport towns,
The weight of his hand held hard the downs.

And the merchants cursed him, bitter and black,
For a red flame in the sea-fog's wrack
Was all of their ships that might come back.

For all he had one word alone,
One clod of dirt in their faces thrown,
"The hemp that shall hang me is not grown!"

[9]

His name bestrode the seas like Death,
The waters trembled at his breath.

This is the tale of how he fell,
Of the long sweep and the heavy swell,
And the rope that dragged him down to hell.

The fight was done, and the gutted ship,
Stripped like a shark the sea-gulls strip,

Lurched blindly, eaten out with flame,
Back to the land from whence she came,
A skimming horror, an eyeless shame.

And Hawk stood up on his quarter-deck,
And saw the sky and saw the wreck.

Below, a butt for sailors' jeers,
White as the sky when a white squall nears,
Huddled the crowd of the prisoners.

Over the bridge of the tottering plank,
Where the sea shook and the gulf yawned blank,
They shrieked and struggled and dropped and sank.

Pinioned arms and hands bound fast.
One girl alone was left at last.

Sir Henry Gaunt was a mighty lord.
He sat in state at the Council board.

The governors were as naught to him.
From one rim to the other rim

Of his great plantations, flung out wide
Like a purple cloak, was a full month's ride.

Life and death in his white hands lay,
And his only daughter stood at bay,
Trapped like a hare in the toils that day.

He sat at wine in his gold and his lace,
And far away, in a bloody place,
Hawk came near, and she covered her face.

He rode in the fields, and the hunt was brave,
And far away, his daughter gave
A shriek that the seas cried out to hear,
And he could not see and he could not save.

Her white soul withered in the mire
As paper shrivels up in fire,
And Hawk laughed, and he kissed her mouth,
And her body he took for his desire.

THE HEMP

II. The Growing of the Hemp

Sir Henry stood in the manor room,
And his eyes were hard gems in the gloom.

And he said, "Go, dig me furrows five
Where the green marsh creeps like a thing alive—
There at its edge where the rushes thrive."

And where the furrows rent the ground
He sowed the seed of hemp around.

And the blacks shrink back and are sore afraid
At the furrows five that rib the glade,
And the voodoo work of the master's spade.

For a cold wind blows from the marshland near,
And white things move, and the night grows drear,
And they chatter and crouch and are sick with fear.

But down by the marsh, where the grey slaves glean,
The hemp sprouts up, and the earth is seen
Veiled with a tenuous mist of green.

And Hawk still scourges the Caribbees,
And many men kneel at his knees.

Sir Henry sits in his house alone,
And his eyes are hard and dull like stone.

And the waves beat, and the winds roar,
And all things are as they were before.

And the days pass, and the weeks pass,
And nothing changes but the grass.

But down where the fireflies are like eyes,
And the damps shudder, and the mists rise,
The hemp-stalks stand up toward the skies.

And down from the poop of the pirate ship
A body falls, and the great sharks grip.

Innocent, lovely, go in grace!
At last there is peace upon your face.

And Hawk laughs loud as the corpse is thrown,
"The hemp that shall hang me is not grown!"

Sir Henry's face is iron to mark,
And he gazes ever in the dark.

[13]

And the days pass, and the weeks pass,
And the world is as it always was.

But down by the marsh the sickles beam,
Glitter on glitter, gleam on gleam,
And the hemp falls down by the stagnant stream.

And Hawk beats up from the Caribbees,
Swooping to pounce in the Northern seas.

Sir Henry sits sunk deep in his chair,
And white as his hand is grown his hair.

And the days pass, and the weeks pass,
And the sands roll from the hourglass.

But down by the marsh, in the blazing sun,
The hemp is smoothed and twisted and spun.
The rope made, and the work done.

THE HEMP

III. *The Using of the Hemp*

Captain Hawk scourged clean the seas,
(Black is the gap below the plank)
From the Great North Bank to the Caribbees
(Down by the marsh the hemp grows rank)

He sailed in the broad Atlantic track
And the ships that saw him came not back.

Till once again, where the wide tides ran,
He stopped to harry a merchantman.

He bade her stop.   Ten guns spoke true
From her hidden ports, and a hidden crew,
Lacking his great ship through and through.

Dazed and dumb with the sudden death,
He scarce had time to draw a breath

[15]

Before the grappling-irons bit deep
And the boarders slew his crew like sheep.

Hawk stood up straight, his breast to the steel;
His cutlass made a bloody wheel.

His cutlass made a wheel of flame.
They shrank before him as he came.

And the bodies fell in a choking crowd,
And still he thundered out aloud,

"The hemp that shall hang me is not grown!"
They fled at last. He was left alone.

Before his foe Sir Henry stood.
"The hemp is grown and my word made good!"

And the cutlass clanged with a hissing whir
On the lashing blade of the rapier.

Hawk roared and charged like a maddened buck.
As the cobra strikes, Sir Henry struck,

Pouring his life in a single thrust,
And the cutlass shivered to sparks and dust.

Sir Henry stood on the blood-stained deck,
And set his foot on his foe's neck.

Then, from the hatch, where the torn decks slope,
Where the dead roll and the wounded grope,
He dragged the serpent of the rope.

The sky was blue and the sea was still,
The waves lapped softly, hill on hill,
And between one wave and another wave
The doomed man's cries were little and shrill.

The sea was blue and the sky was calm,
The air dripped with a golden balm.
Like a wind-blown fruit between sea and sun,
A black thing writhed at a yard-arm.

Slowly then, and awesomely,
The ship sank, and the gallows-tree,
And there was nought between sea and sun—
Nought but the sun and the sky and the sea.

But down by the marsh, where the fever breeds,
Only the water chuckles and pleads;
For the hemp clings fast to a dead man's throat,
And blind Fate gathers back her seeds.

THE MOUNTAIN WHIPPOORWILL

OR, HOW HILL-BILLY JIM WON THE GREAT FIDDLERS' PRIZE

(*A Georgia Romance*)

Up in the mountains, it's lonesome all the time,
(Sof' win' slewin' thu' the sweet-potato vine).

Up in the mountains, it's lonesome for a child,
(Whippoorwills a-callin' when the sap runs wild).

Up in the mountains, mountains in the fog,
Everythin's as lazy as an old houn' dog.

Born in the mountains, never raised a pet,
Don't want nuthin' an' never got it yet.

Born in the mountains, lonesome-born,
Raised runnin' ragged thu' the cockleburrs and corn.

Never knew my pappy, mebbe never should.
Think he was a fiddle made of mountain laurel-wood.

Never had a mammy to teach me pretty-please.
Think she was a whippoorwill, a-skitin' thu' the trees.

Never had a brother ner a whole pair of pants,
But when I start to fiddle, why, yuh got to start to dance!

Listen to my fiddle—Kingdom Come—Kingdom Come!
Hear the frogs a-chunkin' "Jug o' rum, Jug o' rum!"
Hear that mountain-whippoorwill be lonesome in the air,
An' I'll tell yuh how I traveled to the Essex County Fair.

Essex County has a mighty pretty fair,
All the smarty fiddlers from the South come there.

Elbows flyin' as they rosin up the bow
For the First Prize Contest in the Georgia Fiddlers' Show.

Old Dan Wheeling, with his whiskers in his ears,
King-pin fiddler for nearly twenty years.

Big Tom Sargent, with his blue wall-eye,
An' Little Jimmy Weezer that can make a fiddle cry.

All sittin' roun', spittin' high an' struttin' proud,
(Listen, little whippoorwill, yuh better bug yore eyes!)
Tun-a-tun-a-tunin' while the jedges told the crowd
Them that got the mostest claps'd win the bestest prize.

Everybody waitin' for the first tweedle-dee,
When in comes a-stumblin'—hill-billy me!

Bowed right pretty to the jedges an' the rest,
Took a silver dollar from a hole inside my vest,

[19]

Plunked it on the table an' said, "There's my callin' card!
An' anyone that licks me—well, he's got to fiddle hard!"

Old Dan Wheeling, he was laughin' fit to holler,
Little Jimmy Weezer said, "There's one dead dollar!"

Big Tom Sargent had a yaller-toothy grin,
But I tucked my little whippoorwill spang underneath my
    chin,
An' petted it an' tuned it till the jedges said, "Begin!"

Big Tom Sargent was the first in line;
He could fiddle all the bugs off a sweet-potato vine.
He could fiddle down a possum from a mile-high tree.
He could fiddle up a whale from the bottom of the sea.

Yuh could hear hands spankin' till they spanked each
    other raw,
When he finished variations on "Turkey in the Straw."

Little Jimmy Weezer was the next to play;
He could fiddle all night, he could fiddle all day.

He could fiddle chills, he could fiddle fever,
He could make a fiddle rustle like a lowland river.

He could make a fiddle croon like a lovin' woman.
An' they clapped like thunder when he'd finished
    strummin'.

Then came the ruck of the bob-tailed fiddlers,
The let's go-easies, the fair-to-middlers.

They got their claps an' they lost their bicker,
An' settled back for some more corn-licker.

An' the crowd was tired of their no-count squealing,
When out in the center steps Old Dan Wheeling.

He fiddled high and he fiddled low,
(Listen, little whippoorwill; yuh got to spread yore wings!)
He fiddled with a cherrywood bow.
(Old Dan Wheeling's got bee-honey in his strings.)

He fiddled the wind by the lonesome moon,
He fiddled a most almighty tune.

He started fiddling like a ghost,
He ended fiddling like a host.

He fiddled north an' he fiddled south,
He fiddled the heart right out of yore mouth.

He fiddled here an' he fiddled there.
He fiddled salvation everywhere.

When he was finished, the crowd cut loose,
(Whippoorwill, they's rain on yore breast.)
An' I sat there wonderin', "What's the use?"
(Whippoorwill, fly home to yore nest.)

But I stood up pert an' I took my bow,
An' my fiddle went to my shoulder, so.

An'—they wasn't no crowd to get me fazed—
But I was alone where I was raised.

Up in the mountains, so still it makes yuh skeered.
Where God lies sleepin' in his big white beard.

An' I heard the sound of the squirrel in the pine,
An' I heard the earth a-breathin' thu' the long night-time.

They've fiddled the rose, an' they've fiddled the thorn,
But they haven't fiddled the mountain-corn.

They've fiddled sinful an' fiddled moral,
But they haven't fiddled the breshwood-laurel.

They've fiddled loud, an' they've fiddled still,
But they haven't fiddled the whippoorwill.

I started off with a *dump-diddle-dump*,
(*Oh, hell's broke loose in Georgia!*)
Skunk-cabbage growin' by the bee-gum stump,
(*Whippoorwill, yo're singin' now!*)

Oh, Georgia booze is mighty fine booze,
The best yuh ever poured yuh,
But it eats the soles right offen yore shoes,
For Hell's broke loose in Georgia.

My mother was a whippoorwill pert,
My father, he was lazy,
But I'm Hell broke loose in a new store shirt
To fiddle all Georgia crazy.

Swing yore partners—up an' down the middle!
Sashay now—oh, listen to that fiddle!
Flapjacks flippin' on a red-hot griddle,

An' hell broke loose,
Hell broke loose,
Fire on the mountains—snakes in the grass.
Satan's here a-bilin'—oh, Lordy, let him pass!
Go down Moses, set my people free,
Pop goes the weasel thu' the old Red Sea!
Jonah sittin' on a hickory-bough,
Up jumps a whale—an' where's yore prophet now?
Rabbit in the pea-patch, possum in the pot,
Try an' stop my fiddle, now my fiddle's gettin' hot!
Whippoorwill, singin' thu' the mountain hush,
Whippoorwill, shoutin' from the burnin' bush,
Whippoorwill, cryin' in the stable-door,
Sing to-night as yuh never sang before!
Hell's broke loose like a stompin' mountain-shoat,
Sing till yuh bust the gold in yore throat!
Hell's broke loose for forty miles aroun'
Bound to stop yore music if yuh don't sing it down.
Sing on the mountains, little whippoorwill,
Sing to the valleys, an' slap 'em with a hill,
For I'm struttin' high as an eagle's quill,
An' Hell's broke loose,
Hell's broke loose,
Hell's broke loose in Georgia!

They wasn't a sound when I stopped bowin',
(*Whippoorwill, yuh can sing no more.*)
But, somewhere or other, the dawn was growin',
(*Oh, mountain whippoorwill!*)

An' I thought, "I've fiddled all night an' lost.
Yo're a good hill-billy, but yuh've been bossed."

So I went to congratulate old man Dan,
—But he put his fiddle into my han'—
An' then the noise of the crowd began.

[23]

MOON-ISLAND

*(Deposition of Christopher Hew,
the Last American Pirate)*

WHEN we first sighted land
How it made our hearts thunder
To think of new plunder
Dropped into our hand!
When we first sighted land.

It was Midsummer Day
When we let go the anchor,
But the sun had no rancor
Within that calm bay.

We rowed to its shores
With our muskets beside us
And a devil to ride us
With red-hot moidores.

[24]

But the beach was so white,
And the slow minutes crept,
And the hot devil slept,
And the moon rose, in light,

Frail as nautilus shell,
And somehow—in our souls—
We forgot we were coals
Half rejected by hell.

We had come there to loot,
But we sprawled and grew tame there.
And brown women came there
With baskets of fruit.

Fruit cold as moonshine
With a strange taste, and sweet,
With a taste that could beat
Any Portugal wine.

They kept singing a tune,
And we ate—and we gaped—
For each fruitseed was shaped
Like a little new moon.

2

Then we drowsed without care
For our devil was gone,
And the singing kept on,
And the moon filled the air.

And we did not go back
To our ship in the bay,
To our old bird of prey
Where the Roger flapped slack,
And we had the arrack.

No, we lingered and stayed,
And time passed like the sleep
Yellow emperors keep
In their coffins of jade,

While we swam in the pool
Or we played knucklebones
Or we skipped little stones
Like boys out of school.

By the gold hands of day
And the silver of night
We were coins scoured bright
And our sins fell away.

We were wasps without stings,
We were children again there.
Oh, we could have been men there!
We could have been kings.

3

On the last night of all
The moon was at full,
And we heard the tide pull
At the beach's pale shawl.

And the moonseeds had grown
As the moon grew in size,
Till like round silver eyes
In the dark fruit they shone.

And we ate, and the tune
That the brown women sang
Gathered and rang
In a heathenish croon,

As we tossed out the seeds
For the moonbeams to bleach
On the long, burnished beach
Like a goddess's beads.

And then—was it a dream
Or the wine of the fruit?
The moonseeds took root
Where the light made them gleam.

And the roots grew and swelled
And were quickened to vine
In the opal-bright shine,
And we, gasping, beheld

A great Moonvine of pearl
Burgeon under our eyes.
And we saw it arise,
And we saw it uncurl,

An ivory fret,
A glittering stair
Of cold crystal and air,
And the end was not yet.

The brown women's tune
Chanted deeper and deeper.
We saw the pearl creeper
Lay hold of the Moon!

Then the wild song was ended
And we held our breath.
And, in silence like death,
The White Moon descended.

And first she was far
As Heaven is far.
And then she was far
As mortal things are.

And first she was round
And then ghostly with pearl,
And then she was a girl
And stepped to the ground.

She was milk of the pearl.
She was naked as light.
She was fire in the night,
White fire of the pearl.
And—she was a girl.

4

Then the women, light-drowned,
Knelt, covering their eyes,
And the radiant skies
Gave a clear, silver sound.

When someone—not I—
No—not I—but some other—
I swear it! O Mother
Of Mercies, not I!

Came crawling the track
Of an Indian asp
With a gun in his clasp
Behind her white back.

There was sand in the pan,
And the priming was damp.
And she burned like a lamp.
But he was a man.

Like hoarfrost she shined,
Like new sails in the sun,
But he raised the clubbed gun
And struck—from behind.
And then we were blind.

5

There was not a sound.
There was not a spark.
But we lay on the ground
Like bones in the dark.

In a darkness more black
Than ebony-stone,
We lay there alone
And felt our hearts crack.

[29]

Till the dawn rose in blood
And we rose without speech,
And we saw that the beach
Was the color of blood.

And we got to our boat
Without speech, and gave way
For the ship, where she lay
Like a dead man afloat.

And we got the sails set
And went out with the wind.
And the isle fell behind
But we could not forget.

How could we forget,
When we lay down to rest,
And Night bared her black breast,
And no moon rose or set?

The night came too soon.
We could live, in the sun.
But it sank and was done,
And there was not a moon.
There was never a moon.

Only darkness, clay-cold
As a snake, sucking strength—
When you caught us at length
We were madmen grown old.

[30]

But my madness is gone,
And I know where I've been.
I know what I've seen,
And I know when I'm done.

Tell Kidd to move over
His brimstone-and-rum,
For we'll be the clover
Of Hell when we come.

You hangman of tailors,
Here's Satan's doubloon!
Silk rope for the sailors
That murdered the Moon!

II CHARIOTS AND HORSEMEN

THE FIRST VISION OF HELEN

ARGUMENT—*Itys, nurtured by centaurs, meets and falls in love with Helen of Troy, before her marriage with Menelaus. What befell therefrom.*

SLOWLY blanch-handed Dawn, eyes half-awake,
Upraised magnificent the silver urn,
Heaped with white roses at the trembling lip,
Flowers that burn with crystalline accord
And die not ever. Like a pulsing heart
Beat from within against the fire-loud verge
A milky vast transparency of light
Heavy with drowning stars; a swimming void   *Morning.*
Of august ether, formless as the cloud,
And light made absolute. The mountains sighed,
Turning in sleep. Dawn held the frozen flame
An instant high above the shaggy world,
Then, to the crowing of a thousand cocks,
Poured out on earth the unconquerable sun!

The centaurs awoke! they aroused from their beds of pine,
Their long flanks hoary with dew, and their eyes, deep-
    drowned

[35]

In the primal slumber of stones, stirred bright to the shine!
And they stamped with their hooves and their gallop
    abased the ground!

The   Swifter than arrowy birds in an eager sky,
Running White-browed kings of the hills where old Titans feast,
of the   —Cheiron ordered the charge with a neighing cry,
Centaurs. And the thousand hunters tramped like a single beast!

Beautiful monstrous dreams they seemed as they ran,
Trees come alive at the nod of a god grown mute,
Their eyes looked up to the sun like a valiant man;
Their bows clashed shrill on the loins and limbs of the
    brute,

Laughing, rejoicing, white as a naked birch,
Slim as a spear in a torrent of moving towers,
Itys, the prince, ran gay in the storm of their search,
Silverly shod on feet that outstripped the Hours!

    Over by Sparta bays a horn!
    Ohé, Helena!
    Over by Sparta bays a horn!
    And the black hound grins to his milk-teeth torn;
    And the tall stag wishes he'd never been born!
    Helena hunts on the hills!

    Past the Eurotas the chase sweeps hot!
    Ohé, Helena!
    Past the Eurotas the chase sweeps hot!
    And the pack has nosed at a royal slot!
    And a white-armed girl has a magic lot!
    Helena hunts on the hills!

Echoed at Elis the dogs give tongue!
Ohé, Helena!
Echoed at Elis the dogs give tongue!
The stag flees on but his mort is sung,
And the world and Helen are very young!
Helena hunts on the hills!

Down by Argos the flight is stayed!
Ohé, Helena!
Down by Argos the flight is stayed!
And proud blood stifles the reeking blade,
And they cut the tongue for the golden maid!
Helena hunts on the hills!

Over in Troy by a kingly door,
Ohé, Helena!
Over in Troy by a kingly door,
Hector's sword is asleep from war.
"Wait!" whines the bitter steel. "Two years
    more!"
Helena hunts on the hills!

So the two molten clamors fused a space
As silver marries brass to make a bell,
Then thrust apart and vanished, save for some
Faint interlocking tentacles of sound
That chimed to Itys. Something halted him
From the swift gallop and the embracing air,
Put in him troubling languor, drove him out
To rest beside a round coin of a pool,
Casually flung among a cloud of pines.
He dreamed as a dog dreams, uneasily.

[37]

The dreams blow North and South.
Pitiless-bright they gleam.
Send, Zeus, a flower across my mouth,
The wing of a silver dream!

Itys
Dreams.

The visions smoke from the deep,
Bannering East and West.
Guide, Zeus, the stumbling old feet of Sleep,
That bring a dream to my breast!

I have gazed in immaculate eyes!
My soul is a flame astream!
Zeus, strike swift from the raging skies,
That I may die with my dream!

He woke and saw two hounds, tugging their leash,
Burst through the covert, and heard laughter bell
Like a clear stream as Helen followed them.

Itys
Beholds
Helen.

They drank, were quiet. Itys stood at gaze;
Seeing in all things one miraculous face,
And how her tunic left one bright breast bare,
And how she smoothed her hair back with one hand. . . .
But very presently he was aware
That someone not himself possessed his voice
And used it now to talk with—babbling words
Foolish and laughable to that still Beauty.

Tempest from the valiant sky,
Music of the shaken reed,
Can a thousand kisses buy
You and April, mine indeed?
Fling the dice and let them lie!

[38]

Not a joy from all your mind
Will you toss me, beggar's dole,
And you never would be kind
Though I kissed your very soul.
Race the coursers up the wind!

Queen of desperate alarms,
Though Destruction be the priest
That must bring me to your arms,
He shall wed our bones at least!
Life was vintage, borage-crowned,
Pour the cup upon the ground!

Vines grow in my garden;
Blossoms a snake in size.
Sun warms and knife-winds harden,
Till the silk-stained globes arise;
And men peer over the hedges
With fury come in their eyes.

Pears grow in my garden;
Honey a wild bee clips.
Robbers afraid of pardon,
The princes steal from their ships,
And pluck the fruit of iniquity
And take it not from their lips.

Fate grows in my garden;
Black as a cypress shoot.
Sleepily smiles the warden,
Guarding the gorgeous loot,
Seeing the Tree, Deliciousness,
And the tall lords dead at its root.

Itys'
Song.

Helen's
Song.

[39]

Their lips broke from the kiss. Helena sighed,
Then started up, afraid. Straight toward the pool
Rending the brake with hounds, shouting aloud,

The Death Crashed like a cast spear the returning chase.
of Itys. "Itys!" she said. "My brothers. They will kill."
He looked down at his hands that held no sword.
Helena's hounds belled answer to their pack.
Swift as a closing hand, unreal as dream,
Danger shut down around them.

                          "Dear" he said.
Pollux, the shining-speared, burst through the leaves.

After the slaying, wide-eyed Helen paused
To clasp the dead hands loosely, and unhook
A swaying badge of gold from the white neck
That it might burn, a sun, between her breasts.
—The chase passed with hot noon, and in the cool
A straying centaur came, snuffed the new blood,
And, seeing Itys dead, neighed in loud fear;
Calling the hairy tramplers of the woods
To mourn their friend with strange solemnities.

Close his eyes with the coins; bind his chin with the
    shroud;
Death- Carry this clay along, in the time of the westing cloud.
Chant of Lay you the cakes beside, for the three-mouthed dog of
the   Hell;
Centaurs. Slain on the grass in fight, surely his end is well.

Love was the wind he sought, ignorant whence it went;
Now he has clasped it close, silent and eloquent;
Slow as the stream and strong, answering knee to knee,
Carry this clay along—it is more wise than we.

The chanting died away upon the hills,
Sobbingly low.

             And Night reversed the urn;   *Night.*
Drawing all sunlight back to the hot deeps,
And leaving the high heavens full of stars.

THE LAST VISION OF HELEN

ARGUMENT—*Helen, after the fall of Troy, departs to Egypt with ghostly companions, as in the old tale. She encounters the Sphinx and a marvel is wrought upon her.*

MEASURELESS sand . . . interminable sand . . .

The smooth hide of that yellow lion, Earth,
Ruffled a little and was dark again
Beneath the descending torrents of the night,
Plunging like cobalt from the cliffs of the sky,
Blotting the stiff wedge of each pyramid
With the slow gurgle of a rising wave,
A wave burning with stars. . . .
                                        The Sphinx alone
Couched on her forepaws like a sleepy hound
Under the weight of a caress of rock
And smiled her woman's and chimera's smile
Inexorably, drowned with the savage dark.

The black tide filled the heavens up and ceased,
A little tonguing flame ran on the sand
Bright as a fire of paper, swift and light

As a bird's restless eyes. It rose. It bloomed,
An angry dream before the Sphinx's feet,
The exhalation of a furious thought,
Tall as the ghosts of Heaven's battlements,
The apparition that had once been Troy!

A girl went out in the summer skies,
(*The dice lie white for the throwing!*)
A girl went out in the summer skies
And the sunlight laughed as it kissed her eyes!
(*And the wind of Fate is blowing!*)

*Song of
the City
Troy.*

She was ruddy and gold as a changing leaf
When gilded Autumn gathers the sheaf.

She was lily and pale as a sleeping moth
When the full moon bleaches the skies like cloth.

The grass was glad to be under her shoe,
The poppy proud to be floor unto
The silvering dance of her feet like dew!

. . . But her lord walks chill as a cloud of snow
Where the kings of the earth are bending the bow.

They are roaring the fame of the flying dart,
But he whispers low, in a place apart,
With the evil ice of his freezing heart.

"Helena, Helena, mouth of wine,
Two more days for your sun to shine!

Helena, Helena, mouth of musk,
Two more days and I make you dusk.

Two more nights on your silky bed,
And your lover over it, bloody and dead,
And your body broken as I break bread!"

His lips are writhing, sucking and cold,
His hands are twitching like trees grown old,
He shivers as if he had trod on mold.

The *Golden Queen* at her anchor strains.
(*Sails on the sapphire, snowing.*)
Paris walks on the deck like a man in chains.
(*And the wind of Fate is blowing.*)

He wastes in his love like leaves in a flame,
But his mind is a spear in a dauntless game,
And the face of his doom has a girl's soft name.

The fifty sailors are whetting their swords.
The brown sun beats on the tarry boards.

And Helena skims by the rolling sand
And waves with the fleck of a foam-white hand.

And the blood of Youth pounds hot in the throat
As the long oars lash from the lunging boat.

Richly she came through the leaping green,
Like the shrine of a god, like a sun first seen,
And they cried, "Hurrah for the Golden Queen!"

The white sails soar like a rising gull,
The water spins by the speeding hull.

She smiles with her chin cupped into her hand
At the drowning shadow of fading land
—And Paris shakes like a torching brand.

And Paris crushes her, breath to breath,
And she gives him her honey of love and death.

But chill Menelaus a Fury hath,
He has thawed his hate to a roaring wrath!
He is loosing his hounds on the ocean-path!

The blooms of the years are withered and fall.
(*Dawn—and a red flame crowing.*)
And Time's cracked fingers number them all.
(*And the wind of Fate is blowing.*)

And a wooden horse is trampling Troy
As a hoof-thrust crushes a crumpled toy.

Ruddy and gold where the torches stare
Helena sits in her carven chair.

Lovely and strange as a moonlit cloud—
But her head droops down like a petal bowed.

Beneath her the blood and the wine run deep
—But her eyes are seas more quiet than sleep.

The drunkards brawl and the cup goes round;
But she gives no sign and she makes no sound.

Red Menelaus has poured her drink;
And she does not sip and she does not shrink.

And her mouth is a flower that says, "Depart!"
And the hilt of a knife is under her heart.

The kings of the world have finished their chase,
They dash their wine in the glorious face.

And Paris is dead in a sickly land;
And they wrench the rings from the plume-white
    hand.

They dice for her rings and the game is sweet
And lean Menelaus is smiling sleet.

And the captains chuckle, counting their scars,
For the hosts of the earth have finished their wars
And Helen and Troy are cold as the stars.

Waves in the dusk with a sound like tears
(*And the deep tide foaming and flowing.*)
Saying one name for a thousand years!
(*And the wind of Fate is blowing!*)

Like air beaten by swords, like the long cry
Of an old trumpet harsh with rust and gold,
The ballad rose assaulting, struck and died
Into a clamorous echo.
                    The Sphinx stirred,
Shaking the drifted moonlight from her coat
As a dog shakes water, rising mountainously;
Then from that drum of terrible stone, her throat,
Rolled back her answer at the enormous sky.

The arrow of Eros flies
In the dark, in the trembling dark;
Piercing and sweet is the song it cries
And the cup of the heart its mark!
And the cup of the heart is dust,
And the wine of the heart is spilled.
And the barb flings whimpering back to Lust
With "Master, see—I have killed!"
It was thus and thus that you were begot!
I am Death's bright arrow! Forgive me not!

The ribbon of Fate unreels
In the road of the days and nights;
There are flute-voiced airs for the dancing heels,
But over them hang the kites!
And the path grows dark as the laws
And the kites drop down in a ring,
Till a blind stag torn by the slashing claws
Is the end of the trumpeting!
It is there and there that your fathers rot!
I am Destiny's halter! Unloose me not!

The mirror of Wisdom shines
Like a face in a troubled pool.
Like the eyes of a snake are its weaving signs
To the eyes of the anxious fool.
For the secret form of the soul
Is there in its terror shown
—And it rends the sight like a burning coal
Till the eyes of the fool are stone!
It was this and this that your ardor sought!
I am Wisdom's mirror! Behold me not!

[47]

Then, like a forgotten tumult of the heart,
The multitude of men who died for Helen,
Vague, terrible, wounded forms began to chant.

Glance at us once from your sacred tower,
Helen divine!
The cutworm crawls in the almond-flower,
The rats are eating the thrones of power,
Yet glance at us once and the clouds will shower
Our lips with wine!

Loosen your hair to the storm again,
To the whistling brine!
We are very desperate men,
Reeds when fire goes over the fen,
Lighten our dark with your marvel then,
Helen divine!

Give us drink for our bitter thirst,
Helen divine!
Bless you the thieves that each priest has cursed,
Queen of us, queen of us, last and first,
Flame we followed and child we nursed,
Star at trine!

Open the heaven of your embrace,
O burning sign!
This is the end of the bloody race,
Whispering sea and the stars like lace,
You gather our souls to your shining place,
Helen divine!

[48]

The thunder ebbed away into a sigh,
Died into sand, was calm.
                                    And suddenly
Helen of anguish, Helen of the song,
Helen the victory on the lips of Zeus,
Helen the princely word, the proud despair,
The voiceless cry of the ecstatic dream,
Shone with the radiance of a consuming wish
Upon the desert, and stretched out her arms
As if to take that whole great ghost of Troy,
Pennon and panoply, champion and car,
Back to its home, her breast.

Would there ever be a bud   *Helen's*
If the sap considered storm?   *Song.*
It would stay in happy mud,
Damned and sleepy, safe and warm.
Who would want to be a rose
If its petals thought of snows?

Why I lived I never knew.
Life—I took it like a toy,
Something like a worship, too,
To adore and to enjoy.
Then the gods began to play
—And the toy was put away.

Like a perfume made intense,
Like the planet of a dark,
I became magnificence
For my hour, in my spark.
There is rapture in my ghost,
Telling all my least and most.

[49]

Fate and Wisdom, judging loud,
These are shadows I can mock
With the thoughtlessness of cloud,
With the indolence of rock.
Let them air the inn they keep!
I am tired. I would sleep.

So, with the pause, all earth and sky were still
As if they had just been made—and the Sphinx lay
Silent, engulfed in silence.
                              Then she moved
Uneasily, and settled back again,
And in a low harshness of diminished sound
Spoke out her final judgment.

Zeus of the silver dawning took the scarf of a cloud,
He quickened the wraith with fire till the life cried out
    aloud,
He called Desire from his lightning, Despair from her
    weaving old,
And they fashioned the shape to a woman that men might
    die to behold!

*The
Last Song
of the
Sphinx.*
Golden Zeus of the sunbeam slapped his hand on his thigh
As the swords ran out of their scabbards and the arrows
    sang in the sky,
And the woman like leafy April was the chant that an
    archer sings
Over sands grown bloody with purple that has come from
    the hearts of kings.

Zeus of the brazen twilight, nodding his eyes awake,
Armed him a doom for Helen lest Earth burn up for her
    sake;

[50]

Chill on the heart of incense, the hands that desired so
        much,
Fell the snow-like veil of his wisdom, till the flesh was still
        at its touch.

Iron Zeus of the night-time, watching the chariot moon
Trample the skies to whiteness, turns like a moving dune
To gaze at the shade of Helen. His eyes as the skies are
        vast;
Seeing her sleep like a swallow in Death's wide bed at last.

                                        Helen stood
        Within the tremendous circle of the paws,
        Moving like light towards the dark secret heart.
        The Sphinx cried terribly with a wordless sound
        Of birth and anguish struggling to be heard . . .
        And the light vanished . . .
                                And Helen and the Sphinx
        Were one forever, stone and ghost and dream—
        And Troy was gone like vapor in the dark.

        So the dawn came, and toiling caravans,
        Whose princes halted, arrogant as hawks,
        To stare but once into the Sphinx's eyes
        . . . And so were staring till Death breathed on them
        With the slant feathers of his ruffling wing,
        Seeking within the rock, the stubborn rock,
        The gaze and burning of their Lost Desire.

WINGED MAN

THE moon, a sweeping scimitar, dipped in the stormy
    straits,
The dawn, a crimson cataract, burst through the eastern
    gates,
The cliffs were robed in scarlet, the sands were cinnabar,
Where first two men spread wings for flight and dared
    the hawk afar.

There stands the cunning workman, the crafty past all
    praise,
The man who chained the Minotaur, the man who built
    the Maze.
His young son is beside him and the boy's face is a light,
A light of dawn and wonder and of valor infinite.

Their great vans beat the cloven air, like eagles they
    mount up,
Motes in the wine of morning, specks in a crystal cup,

And lest his wings should melt apace old Dædalus flies
  low,
But Icarus beats up, beats up, he goes where lightnings go.

He cares no more for warnings, he rushes through the sky,
Braving the crags of ether, daring the gods on high,
Black 'gainst the crimson sunrise, golden o'er cloudy
  snows,
With all Adventure in his heart the first winged man
  arose.

Dropping gold, dropping gold, where the mists of morning
  rolled,
On he kept his way undaunted, though his breaths were
  stabs of cold,
Through the mystery of dawning that no mortal may
  behold.

Now he shouts, now he sings in the rapture of his wings,
And his great heart burns intenser with the strength of
  his desire,
As he circles like a swallow, wheeling, flaming, gyre on
  gyre.

Gazing straight at the sun, half his pilgrimage is done,
And he staggers for a moment, hurries on, reels back-
  ward, swerves
In a rain of scattered feathers as he falls in broken curves.

Icarus, Icarus, though the end is piteous,
Yet forever, yea, forever we shall see thee rising thus,
See the first supernal glory, not the ruin hideous.

You were Man, you who ran farther than our eyes can
scan,
Man absurd, gigantic, eager for impossible Romance,
Overthrowing all Hell's legions with one warped and
broken lance.

On the highest steeps of Space he will have his dwelling-
place,
In those far, terrific regions where the cold comes down
like Death
Gleams the red glint of his pinions, smokes the vapor of
his breath.

Floating downward, very clear, still the echoes reach the
ear
Of a little tune he whistles and a little song he sings,
Mounting, mounting still, triumphant, on his torn and
broken wings!

THE RETORT DISCOURTEOUS

(*Italy—16th Century*)

BUT what, by the fur on your satin sleeves,
The rain that drags at my feather
And the great Mercurius, god of thieves,
Are we thieves doing together?

Last night your blades bit deep for their hire,
And we were the sickled barley.
To-night, atoast by the common fire,
You ask me to join your parley.

Your spears are shining like Iceland spar,
The blood-grapes drip for your drinking;
For you folk follow the rising star,
I follow the star that's sinking!

My queen is old as the frosted whins,
Nay, how could her wrinkles charm me?
And the starving bones are bursting the skins
In the ranks of her ancient army.

[55]

You marshal a steel-and-silken troop,
Your cressets are fed with spices,
And you batter the world like a rolling hoop
To the goal of your proud devices.

I have rocked your thrones—but your fight is won.
To-night, as the highest bidder,
You offer a share of your brigand-sun,
Consider, old bull, consider!

Ahead, red Death and the Fear of Death,
Your vultures, stoop to the slaughter.
But I shall fight you, body and breath,
Till my life runs out like water!

My queen is wan as the Polar snows.
Her host is a rout of specters.
But I gave her Youth like a burning rose,
And her age shall not lack protectors!

I would not turn for the thunderclap
Or the face of the woman who bore me,
With her battered badge still scarring my cap,
And the drums of defeat before me.

Roll your hands in the honey of life,
Kneel to your white-necked strumpets!
You came to your crowns with a squealing fife
But I shall go out with trumpets!

Poison the steel of the plunging dart,
Holloa your hounds to their station!
I march to my ruin with such a heart
As a king to his coronation.

Your poets roar of your golden feats—
I have herded the stars like cattle.
And you may die in the perfumed sheets,
But I shall die in battle.

ALEXANDER VI DINES
WITH THE CARDINAL OF CAPUA

Next, then, the peacock, gilt
With all its feathers. Look, what gorgeous dyes
Flow in the eyes!
And how deep, lustrous greens are splashed and spilt
Along the back, that like a sea-wave's crest
Scatters soft beauty o'er th' emblazoned breast!

A strange fowl! But most fit
For feasts like this, whereby I honor one
Pure as the sun!
Yet glowing with the fiery zeal of it!
Some wine? Your goblet's empty? Let it foam!
It is not often that you come to Rome.

You like the Venice glass?
Rippled with lines that float like women's curls,
Neck like a girl's,
Fierce-glowing as a chalice in the Mass?

You start—'twas artist then, not Pope who spoke!
Ave Maria stella!—ah, it broke!

'Tis said they break alone
When poison writhes within. A foolish tale!
What, you look pale?
Caraffa, fetch a silver cup! . . . You own
A Birth of Venus, now—or so I've heard,
Lovely as the breast-plumage of a bird.

Also a Dancing Faun,
Hewn with the lithe grace of Praxiteles;
Globed pearls to please
A sultan; golden veils that drop like lawn—
How happy I could be with but a tithe
Of your possessions, fortunate one! Don't writhe

But take these cushions here!
Now for the fruit! Great peaches, satin-skinned,
Rough tamarind,
Pomegranates red as lips—oh they come dear!
But men like you we feast at any price—
A plum perhaps? They're looking rather nice.

I'll cut the thing in half.
There's yours! Now, with a one-side-poisoned knife
One might snuff life
And leave one's friend with—"fool" for epitaph.
An old trick? Truth! But when one has the itch
For pretty things and isn't very rich. . . .

[59]

There, eat it all or I'll
Be angry! You feel giddy? Well, it's hot!
This bergamot
Take home and smell—it purges blood of bile;
And when you kiss Bianca's dimpled knee,
Think of the poor Pope in his misery!

Now you may kiss my ring.
Ho there, the Cardinal's litter!—You must dine
When the new wine
Is in, again with me—hear Bice sing,
Even admire my frescoes—though they're nought
Beside the calm Greek glories you have bought.

Godspeed, Sir Cardinal,
And take a weak man's blessing! Help him there
To the cool air! . . .
Lucrezia here? You're ready for the ball?
—He'll die within ten hours, I suppose—
MhM! Kiss your poor old father, little rose!

THREE DAYS' RIDE

"From Belton Castle to Solway side,
Hard by the bridge, is three days' ride."

We had fled full fast from her father's keep,
And the time was come that we must sleep.

The first day was an ecstasy,
A golden mist, a burgeoning tree;
We rode like gods through a world new-made,
The hawthorn scented hill and glade,
A faint, still sweetness in the air—
And, oh, her face and the wind in her hair!
And the steady beat of our good steeds' hooves,
Bearing us northward, strong and fast,
To my high black tower, stark to the blast,
Like a swimmer stripped where the Solway moves.

And ever, riding, we chanted a song,
Challenging Fortune, loud and long,
"From Belton Castle to Solway side,
Strive as you may, is three days' ride!"

She slept for an hour, wrapped in my cloak,
And I watched her till the morning broke;
The second day—and a harsher land,
And grey bare hills on either hand;
A surly land and a sullen folk,
And a fog that came like bitter smoke.

The road wound on like a twisted snake,
And our horses sobbed as they topped the brake.
Till we sprang to earth at Wyvern Fen,
Where fresh steeds stamped, and were off again.
Weary and sleepless, bruised and worn,
We still had strength for laughter and scorn;
Love held us up through the mire and mist,
Love fed us, while we clasped and kissed,
And still we sang as the night closed in,
Stealthy and slow as a hidden sin,
"From Belton Castle to Solway side,
Ride how you will, is three days' ride."

My love drooped low on the black mare's back,
Drowned in her hair . . . the reins went slack . . .
Yet she could not sleep, save to dream bad dreams
And wake all trembling, till at last
Her golden head lay on my breast.

At last we saw the first faint gleams
Of day. Dawn broke. A sickly light
Came from the withered sun—a blight

[62]

Was on the land, and poisonous mist
Shrouded the rotting trees, unkissed
By any wind, and black crags glared
Like sightless, awful faces, spared
From death to live accursed for aye.

Dragging slow chains the hours went by.
We rode on, drunk and drugged with sleep,
Too deadly weary now to say
Whether our horses kept the way
Or no—like slaves stretched on a heap
Of poisoned arrows. Every limb
Shot with sharp pain; pain seemed to swim
Like a red cloud before our eyes. . . .

The mist broke, and a moment showed,
Sharp as the Devil's oxen-goad,
The spear-points where the hot chase rode.

Idly I watched them dance and rise
Till white wreaths wiped them out again . . .
My love jerked at the bridle rein;
The black mare, dying, broke her heart
In one swift gallop; for my part
I dozed; and ever in my brain,
Four hoofs of fire beat out refrain,
A dirge to light us down to death,
A silly rhyme that saith and saith,
"*From Belton Castle to Solway side,
Though great hearts break, is three days' ride!*"
The black mare staggered, reeled and fell,
Bearing my love down . . . a great bell
Began to toll . . . and sudden fire
Flared at me from the road, a pyre

It seemed, to burn our bodies in . . .
And I fell down, far down, within
The pit's mouth . . . and my brain went blind. . . .

I woke—a cold sun rose behind
Black evil hills—my love knelt near
Beside a stream, her golden hair
Streaming across the grass—below
The Solway eddied to and fro,
White with fierce whirlpools . . . my love turned. . . .
Thank God, some hours of joy are burned
Into the mind, and will remain,
Fierce-blazing still, in spite of pain!

They came behind us as we kissed,
Stealthily from the dripping mist,
Her brothers and their evil band.
They bound me fast and made me stand.
They forced her down upon her knees.
She did not strive or cry or call,
But knelt there dumb before them all—
I could not turn away my eyes—
There was no fear upon her face,
Although they slew her in that place.
The daggers rent and tore her breast
Like dogs that snarl above a kill,
Her proud face gazed above them still,
Seeking rest—Oh, seeking rest!
The blood swept like a crimson dress
Over her bosom's nakedness,
A curtain for her weary eyes,
A muffling-cloth to stop her sighs . . .
And she was gone—and a red thing lay
Silent, on the trampled clay.

Beneath my horse my feet are bound,
My hands are bound behind my back,
I feel the sinews start and crack—
And ever to the hoof-beats' sound,
As we draw near the gallows-tree,
Where I shall hang right speedily,
A crazy tune rings in my brain,
Four hoofs of fire tramp the refrain,
Crashing clear o'er the roaring crowd,
Steadily galloping, strong and loud,
"From Belton Castle to Solway side,
Hard by the bridge, is three days' ride!"

CAROL: NEW STYLE

If **Jesus Christ** *should come again,*
On Christmas day, on Christmas day,
To bother the minds of gentlemen
On Christmas day in the morning?

The first one said as he passed by,
As he passed by, as he passed by,
"I see three thieves a-hanging high,
This Christmas day in the morning."

The second one said, "What sinful men!
What sinful men, what sinful men!
Hanging is too good for them,
On Christmas day in the morning."

The third one said, "Oh stay your word!
Stay your word, oh stay your word!
Do you not see that one's the Lord,
This Christmas day in the morning?"

"I know him by his weary head,
His weary head, his weary head."
Whereat they all fell sore adread,
That Christmas day in the morning.

"How sad this is we all avow,
Yes indeed, we all avow!
But what shall we do about it now,
On Christmas day in the morning?"

PRIMUS

"I'll run away as fast as I may,
As fast as I may, as fast as I may,
And pretend I haven't been out all day,
On Christmas day in the morning."

SECUNDUS

"I'll buy Him a shroud that's spick and span,
Spick and span, spick and span,
For I was always a generous man,
On Christmas day in the morning."

TERTIUS

"But what if we should cut Him down,
Cut Him down, cut Him down?"

SECUNDUS ET PRIMUS

"You fool, do you want to arouse the town,
On Christmas day in the morning?"

"My speech was rash," the third one said,
The third one said, the third one said.
"We're surer of God when we know He's dead,
On any day in the morning."

They knelt in the snow and prayed and bowed,
Prayed and bowed, prayed and bowed,
And the two dead thieves laughed out aloud
On Christmas day in the morning.

As Jesus Christ was hanging high,
Hanging high, hanging high,
He saw three Christians, passing by,
On Christmas day in the morning.

III SKYSCRAPER HOUSE

RAIN AFTER A VAUDEVILLE SHOW

THE last pose flickered, failed. The screen's dead white
Glared in a sudden flooding of harsh light
Stabbing the eyes; and as I stumbled out
The curtain rose. A fat girl with a pout
And legs like hams, began to sing "His Mother."
Gusts of bad air rose in a choking smother;
Smoke, the wet steam of clothes, the stench of plush,
Powder, cheap perfume, mingled in a rush.
I stepped into the lobby—and stood still
Struck dumb by sudden beauty, body and will.
Cleanness and rapture—excellence made plain—
The storming, thrashing arrows of the rain!
Pouring and dripping on the roofs and rods,
Smelling of woods and hills and fresh-turned sods,
Black on the sidewalks, grey in the far sky,
Crashing on thirsty panes, on gutters dry,
Hurrying the crowd to shelter, making fair
The streets, the houses, and the heat-soaked air,—
Merciful, holy, charging, sweeping, flashing,

It smote the soul with a most iron clashing! . . .
Like dragons' eyes the street-lamps suddenly gleamed,
Yellow and round and dim, low globes of flame.
And, scarce-perceived, the clouds' tall banners streamed.
Out of the petty wars, the daily shame,
Beauty strove suddenly, and rose, and flowered. . . .
I gripped my coat and plunged where awnings lowered.
Made one with hissing blackness, caught, embraced,
By splendor and by striving and swift haste—
Spring coming in with thunderings and strife—
I stamped the ground in the strong joy of life!

LUNCH-TIME ALONG BROADWAY

TWELVE-THIRTY bells from a thousand clocks, the type-
   writer tacks and stops,
Gorged elevators slam and fall through the floors like
   water-drops,
From offices hung like sea-gulls' nests on a cliff the whirl-
   winds beat,
The octopus-crowd comes rolling out, his tentacles crawl
   for meat.

He snuffles his way by restaurants where lily-voiced
   women feast,
He pokes his muzzle through white-tiled caves, and gulps
   like a hungry beast,
He roots into subterranean holes, he sweeps hell's tables
   bare,
His suckers settle and fix and drink like wasps on a bursting pear.

[73]

The wildcat quarrel of traffic soothes to a smooth rolling
  of tires
And the waterflow sound of the feeding brute as he pads
  by the cooking-fires,
His body shoulders the canyoned streets, his gluttonous
  mouths expand
And he laps the fat and flesh of the earth as a cat laps milk
  from a hand.

Slowly the greedy claws curl back, the feelers recoil and
  close,
The flood is setting the other way with the avalanche
  pound of snows,
Heavy and hot as a sated bee, enormous, slower than oil.
The beast comes shuffling to lair again, his lips still wet
  with his spoil.

THE WALKERS

(Strike Pickets—Lower Fifth Ave.)

IT IS past day and its brilliance, it is not yet sumptuous
    night
For the moon to shine on gardened roofs like a white nut
    peeled of its husk,
The march of the ant-hill crowds below is like sand falling
    from a height,
And the lost horns of the taxis cry hooting through the
    dusk.

Grey as rain in an autumn wood when the skies are pale
    with cloud
Are the light and the street and the faces where the
    elephant busses roll,
Dark motors shine like a seal's wet skin, and they and their
    rich are proud,
But the walkers are dim and aimless on a dolorous way of
    the soul.

[75]

I watch, and my soft, pleased body cries for the rooms with
　　lights like flowers,
For the delicate talk of women, and music's deep-perfumed
　　smart,
And I sweat at the walkers crushed by machining, im-
　　placable hours,
And in torment I turn away—but their march is over my
　　heart.

They are helpless as drifting weed, they are stung with
　　insane impatience
At themselves and their lords and their hunger no toil can
　　feed till it sleeps.
They are racked earth hating the plow, they are dung at
　　the roots of the nations,
They are wheat that will not be bread and burns at the
　　scythe that reaps.

Ensigns of honor they bear not, their songs are ignorant
　　clamors.
I hate their joy and their fear. I am bitter afraid of pain.
But the pitiful tune of their feet is trampling my soul with
　　hammers,
And I must follow them out in the desolate face of the rain.

Ask not watchword nor sign—there is neither tocsin nor
　　clarion;
Only the strength of the flood, the might of the falling
　　snow,
The cry of the bitter clay to the God who devised it carrion,
The purblind silence of sleep, as night to the night we flow.

8:30 A.M. ON 32ND STREET

THE *wind sniffed like a happy cat*
At scuttling beetle-people,
The sunshine would have roused a flat
To try and be a steeple.

My breakfast in me warm and staunch,
Your letter in my pocket,
The world's a coon that's climbed a branch
And I am David Crockett.

Time hoards our lives with griping care
And barren is his bursary,
But he'll make diamonds of the air
Upon one anniversary!

Five years ago I saw you first
And knew in every part
The flagrant and immortal thirst
Love salts into the heart.

Five years ago the Pleiad crew
Sang in their starry hive,
Because a miracle like you
Could dare to be alive.

Five years, and still, through earth's degrees
You, like a pageant, pass;
Courageous as invading seas
And careless as the grass.

Pauper poets of rimes grown thin
Mutter their madhouse wrongs.
I have aeons to love you in,
Ages to make you songs!

Pour your rain on the bitter tree!
Harrow the soil with spears!
I shall grow you Felicity,
After a million years!

The street-signs winked like smiles at me,
The wind pawed by enchanted;
The sun swung high for all to see.
I'd stop him if I wanted!

HYMN IN COLUMBUS CIRCLE

(After Seeing a Certain Window Display)

Man in his secret shrine
Hallows a wealth of gods,
Black little basalt Baals
Wood-kings heard in the pine,
Josses whose jade prevails
Breaking Disaster's rods;
Prayers have made each one shine.

Man's is a pious race.
Once he knelt to the moss,
Ra, Astarte or Jove,
Deities great and base,
—Once his questionings clove
To the stubborn arms of the Cross
That smote all lies in the face.

Here is a new desire,
One of his latest lauds
Throned on marble and praised
With the lovely softness of fire.
Signs acclaim it amazed,
Its window-altar is hazed,
And every gazer applauds
The tremendous rubber tire.

IV KING DAVID

KING DAVID

DAVID sang to his hook-nosed harp:
"The Lord God is a jealous God!
His violent vengeance is swift and sharp!
And the Lord is King above all gods!

"Blest be the Lord, through years untold,
The Lord Who has blessed me a thousand fold!

"Cattle and concubines, corn and hives
Enough to last me a dozen lives.

"Plump, good women with noses flat,
Marrowful blessings, weighty and fat.

"I wax in His peace like a pious gourd,
The Lord God is a pleasant God,
Break mine enemy's jaw, O Lord!
For the Lord is King above all gods!"

His hand dropped slack from the tunable strings,
A sorrow came on him—a sorrow of kings.

A sorrow sat on the arm of his throne,
An eagle sorrow with claws of stone.

"I am merry, yes, when I am not thinking,
But life is nothing but eating and drinking.

"I can shape my psalms like daggers of jade,
But they do not shine like the first I made.

"I can harry the heathen from North to South,
But no hot taste comes into my mouth.

"My wives are comely as long-haired goats,
But I would not care if they cut their throats!

"Where are the maids of the desert tents
With lips like flagons of frankincense?

"Where is Jonathan? Where is Saul?
The captain-towers of Zion wall?

"The trees of cedar, the hills of Nod,
The kings, the running lions of God?

"Their words were a writing in golden dust,
Their names are myrrh in the mouths of the just.

"The sword of the slayer could never divide them—
Would God I had died in battle beside them!"